KT-427-686

Bright
FOR
Early Years

Language Activities

Published by Scholastic Publications Ltd,
Villiers House, Clarendon Avenue,
Leamington Spa, Warwickshire CV32 5PR.

© 1990 Scholastic Publications Ltd
Reprinted 1991, 1995

Written by Irene Yates
Edited by Christine Lee
Sub-edited by Anne Faundez
Cover by Martyn Chillmaid
Designed by Sue Limb
Illustrations by Jane Andrews
Photographs by Isabelle Butchinsky,
taken at Lakey Lane Primary School,
Birmingham
Artwork by Liz Preece,
Castle Graphics, Kenilworth
Printed in Great Britain by
The Alden Press, Oxford

British Library Cataloguing in Publication Data
Bright ideas for early years
    Language activities
    1. Primary schools. Activities
    I. Yates, Irene
    372.19

ISBN 0-590-76297-4

Contents

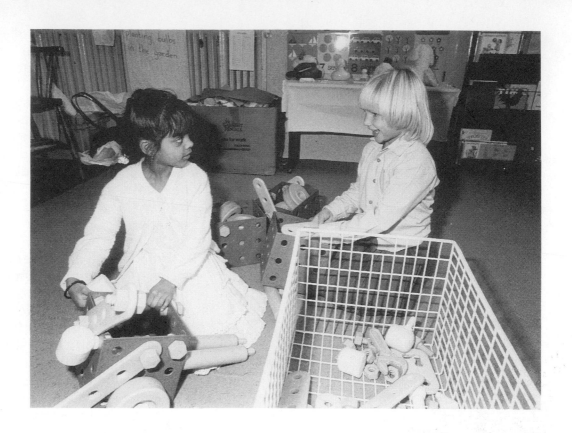

Introduction

Bright Ideas for Early Years Language Activities offers a comprehensive collection of activities which foster language development through use. It suggests a whole-language approach so that children can build up their knowledge of language without specific practice of skills, within their natural environment. In this way, language arises with a purpose and meets the children's own needs.

Writing a book of language activities is not quite as straightforward as writing a book on other areas of the curriculum. To begin with, all activities are language activities. There is no task that does not involve talking and listening, maybe even reading and writing. Current theory is that a child will internalise a word or phrase after hearing and using it in context on average 17 times.

It is important not to fall into the 'labelling' trap: 'This is an orange. What is it? An orange.' Language consists of much more than labels. We want our children to be able to say, 'It's my turn next' or 'I'll go after Anna' with conviction and confidence. Thus there is little use in a language activity book that merely points towards labelling. What I have tried to do here is to guide the reader towards the kind of language one might expect to develop through any of the given activities.

Even though the under-fives are not included in National Curriculum provision, we need to be looking at the attainment targets for Key Stage 1 and beginning to aim towards them. However, the emphasis should always be upon process rather than product; the language the children experience in doing the task is what helps them to develop their own language and thinking skills, not the piece of work that they have to show at the end of the activity.

How children use language

To little children language is as uncomplicated as anything can be. Ask a child what it feels like to be five and she may answer something like, 'It feels easy'. What's easy? 'Easy is when the puppy dog falls asleep curled up on your lap.' If the toaster breaks down, then she comes and tells you that 'the bread just stayed bread this morning'. If you hold out one red sweet in each hand and ask a little child if they are both the same, she'll look at you as if you were daft. How can they be the same (she thinks you mean the same one) when there are two different sweets? In the same way, to her 'different' means 'another one' not 'dissimilar'.

The way to encourage language

development is to get the children talking: you learn to talk by talking, you learn to read by reading, you learn to write by writing and you learn to listen by listening. A child without the opportunity to verbalise, a child who is afraid of making a mistake, is a child who will not talk. Encourage children to talk by surrounding them with experiences that promote language and prompt expression of their thoughts.

Sharing literature

Select big books with interesting rhythms and recurring phrases. Encourage the children to chant along as you read. The children will want to read the stories over and over again. Soon they will begin to match pictures and words, associating certain language with specific pictures; they will begin to rote-read passages, and later they will begin to recognise a few familiar words and phrases. Eventually they will read most of the passage with understanding.

Follow a simple procedure for sharing books with the children. At the beginning of each week:

- Choose a book with a good literary pattern (see appendix).
- Read to the children without showing them the pictures.
- Cut your own large pages, about 30 cm × 45 cm.
- At the top of each page print a part of the story.
- Read the story to the children, tracking each word as you do so.
- Invite the children to join in.
- Invite the children to 'read' while you point, giving them the words they cannot remember.
- Give the children a part of the story to illustrate. Encourage large pictures.
- Put your book together, make a cover and bind it.
- Read the original book to the children, showing them the pictures.
- Using the class book, invite individual children to point to the words whilst the rest 'read' together.
- Invite individuals to read the book. Place the book in the reading corner for leisure reading.
- Choose other books and repeat the procedure each week.

Using a book to greatest advantage

After reading a new book to the children and showing them the pictures, go through it again carefully, pointing out the pictures specifically, using the names of the characters, asking the children what is happening in the picture. This will help them to re-tell the story in their own words and allow them to get the sequence right.

After discussion, read the story again, pausing every now and then so that the children can predict and fill in the words.

Make a 'book-on-the-wall' by making word-strip captions for pictures that the children paint or draw. Get the children to decide on the sequence in which you should display them. Alternatively, use large pieces of card to make a zig-zag book, using the same methods. Instead of having word-strip captions, draw some of the pictures with speech bubbles, allowing the children to decide what should go in each bubble.

Writing

The children should be encouraged to 'write' for themselves. Scribble writing is a very necessary part of the writing development process and you should be able to note and evaluate the following stages:

● Story scribble:
'We went to my nan's. She gave us some ice cream. It was nice.'

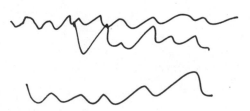

- Sentence scribble: each line of scribble represents a sentence.
'I went to the shops. My mum bought some sweets. I ate all the sweets.'

~~~~~~~~

~~~~~~~~

~~~~~~~~

- Word scribble: each line of scribble represents a word.
'I played with my friend and we stayed up late.'

- Consonant spelling: the child uses letters (not the sound symbol), ie initial consonant spelling, initial and final consonant spelling or a combination of scribble and letters.
'They came back and another man found the dog.'

the cmb and
amun mn faw
the dg

- Invented spelling: the child uses consonant spelling and vowels, and spells some common words correctly. He uses a combination of scribble, invented spellings and correct spellings.

thhe camdc and
anine man fawd
the dog

- Invented spelling and standard spelling: the child uses invented spellings and corrects some himself. He gradually transfers to more standard spelling.

they came bak
and another
man fownd the
dog

It is important to value the marks and squiggles children make at this stage: if you always decode or underwrite their work, children may feel that their efforts are not 'right', not valuable.

To promote intrinsic motivation for writing, encourage the children by:
- trusting in them;
- enjoying and accepting their efforts at every stage;
- providing opportunities for daily writing;
- allowing talk and discussion;
- providing varieties of paper, writing and drawing tools, card etc.

Encouraging talk

As well as being encouraged to develop their own powers of speech, children should learn to develop their listening skills. You can help them with this by reading to them and asking them questions about the stories. Encourage the children to listen to their friends talking about what they are doing, to listen to music and story tapes and to listen to the sounds around them such as running water or birds singing.

Children's descriptive skills can be enhanced by getting them to explain to their families what they have been doing at school, tell their friends about their homes and families and talk about what they are doing, whether they are playing with sand, water, paint or in the toy corner.

Above all, encourage them to talk about themselves. Ask them questions about themselves. What colour hair do you have? Do you know what size shoes you take? Who is your best friend? What do you like best at school? Have you got any pets? Do you have any brothers and sisters? Who brings you to school? What did you have for your lunch? What is your favourite colour? Can you count?

What would you eat at a party? Any question relating to the child's own experiences will help him to formulate sentences with which to express himself.

Encourage the children to look at plenty of books and pictures and to talk about them. Ask parents to help by reading to their children at home and let the children bring their own favourite books from home into the classroom for the rest of the class to look at and discuss.

First experiences

Chapter one

Children starting nursery or playschool may find themselves expected, for the first time, to talk with adults who do not have the same wealth of shared experience (including knowledge, accent, language). They will need you to provide a context they can understand, a real purpose for talking, a responsive listener. They need to perceive their teacher not as a classroom or talk 'manager' but as someone who demonstrates interest in what they have to say. They need time to reflect, time to have another go, time to extend what they think and what they have to say.

Questioning is not an 'easy' option. You have to take care to 'prompt' not 'probe' and not to deflect the children's thought processes and responses by asking another question too soon. Remember that for little children the 'what', 'where' and 'when' answers may come quite easily but the 'how' and the 'why' require a considerable amount of cognitive effort!

Learning the language of school

What you need
No special equipment.

What to do
Take the children for a walk around the school to introduce them to language with which they may be unfamiliar. Start in one corridor and walk all the way through the school, asking the children questions along the way.

Look at the walls. Are there pictures on the walls? Are there stories? Do the walls display lots of work done by the children? How do you think they made the dragon?

Can you see any cupboards? Are there nice things to look at on top of the cupboards? Models? Pottery? Vases of flowers? Perhaps there are some plants. If so, which do you like best?

Perhaps, one day, you can make some models for the corridor cupboards. Maybe you will be able to look after the plants.

Look for doors. Behind each door is a room. In each room somebody works. Whose room do you think this is? Can you get a clue from listening?

Guess what's behind the doors. Can you guess which room has the television inside it? Can you guess which room is the library? Can you guess which room is the staffroom? Are all the doors open? Are all the doors closed? Why should you knock before you go in?

Lots of rooms have notices on them to tell you what they are used for and to whom they belong. You can read the notices yourself. This one announces the secretary's office. This notice says 'Mrs Jones', since this is her classroom.

Can you find the door that visitors come in through? Is it the same door that the children use to come in?

What does the entrance hall look like?
Is it cheerful? Warm and cosy? Or is it
drab and dull? Are there chairs for
people to sit on? What's on the floor? Is
there a carpet? Or tiles? Or is the floor
made of wood? Which do you prefer?

If you were building an entrance hall,
how would you make it pretty and
comfortable to cheer up your visitors?
How could you make sure it kept warm?

Walk through the entrance hall into the
corridors. Listen. Can you hear anything?
What can you hear? Keep your eyes
open, look out for everything you can
see. What can you see?

Do you meet any people along the
way? Say hello to them. Who do you
meet? Where are they going? Are they
noisy or quiet people?

Walk along the corridor. Watch out for
the hall. The hall's a great big room. How
big do you think it is? Do you think it's
very big? Huge? Massive? Enormous?
Bigger than any room you've ever seen
before? Or is it only quite big? A bit
bigger than your bedroom? As big as a
garage? Big enough for an aeroplane?

Stand in the middle of the room and
listen. What can you hear? Can you hear
anything at all? Is there any music
playing? Are there any children
chattering?

Can you hear anything from outside? Is
the wind blowing in the trees? Are the
birds whistling? Are there children in the
playground?

Suppose the hall was full of teddy
bears, what would it sound like then?
What would you hear if there were
hundreds of kittens in here? What if it
were full of elephants? What do you
think it will sound like when you come to
your first school assembly and it's
crammed full of children?

Is there anything to look at in the hall?
Have the children done any work for
display? What kind of work is it? Which is
your favourite piece of work? What

would you like to do that could be put in the hall?

Sometimes people do PE in the hall. Try to find the equipment. Can you see any skipping ropes? Hoops? Bean bags? Can you tell what any of the labels say?

The ropes go in this cupboard

The bean bags go in this cupboard

The hoops go here

Classroom peeping

What you need
No special equipment.

What to do
It is important for the children to know where the other classrooms are as well as the location of facilities they will need to use, such as cloakrooms and toilets.

Ask your colleagues if you can disrupt their classes temporarily while your class goes on its guided tour.

Take a peep into the classrooms. Watch the infant children making models. Listen to them chattering. Ask them if they're having a good day.

Listen to the children in the junior classrooms. Knock on the door before you go in and say hello. Ask them what they're doing. Listen to their chatter. Have a look at their work. Have they got pictures on the walls? Stories?

Talk about the building. Is it a great big place, part of a larger school, or is it self-contained? Is there an outside as well as inside area to play in? What do you call the outside? Is it a playground? What do you call the inside? Is it a classroom? Is it a playschool, or a nursery? Where are the toilets? Where is the cloakroom? What's in the cloakroom? Are there pegs? What do you do with the pegs? Are there any pictures on the pegs? Which picture belongs to you? Which picture belongs to your friend?

How many doors did you see? What does our room look like? Is it cheerful? Warm and cosy? Or is it drab and dull? Are there lots of chairs for people to sit in? Are there tiles on the floor? Is it made of wood or is it carpeted? Which do you think would be best?

Make a picture map

What you need
Paper, card, scissors, adhesive, felt-tipped pens, adhesive tape.

What to do
After taking the children round the school, make pictures of the different areas using pieces of card. Talk about what a map is. When the children understand the task, discuss which areas you want to show on your picture map.

Divide the class into groups and ask each group to make a different part of the map. Ask them for words to write on each part. They may want to write things like 'Mr Smith is our headteacher and this is his room', or 'The children all have their dinner in this big hall'. Write the words for them, getting them to read along with you. If the children want to label bits for themselves, for instance they may like to 'write' the notice on Mr Smith's door, encourage them to do so in their own way and at their own stage of development. Do not insist on writing it 'properly' for them.

When all the parts of the map are ready, stick them together with adhesive tape to make one huge map and display it on a wall. Invite other people to look at the map and encourage the children to share their knowledge and show what they have done, helping them to 'read' and remember the words they have chosen for you to write. Show them, in as many ways as you can, that their work is valued and important.

Introducing ourselves

What you need
Camera, paper, pens, sponge, powder paint, scissors.

What to do
Little children are egocentric, so it makes sense to involve them in a project about themselves.

Take photographs of the children and display them with their names. Encourage them to talk about their physical features, about their likes and dislikes, about their families. Get them to draw themselves and each other and to colour in their hair and eyes as accurately as they can.

Make handprints using a sponge soaked with powder paint, cut the handprints out and display them with photos. How many children are there? How many pairs of hands? How many hands altogether?

Talk about eyes, ears and noses. Talk about the senses, seeing, smelling, tasting, hearing and touching. Give them objects to touch but not see. Can they guess what they are? How do they guess? Give them things to taste on their tongues, things to smell. Can they guess what they are? Can they describe the tastes and textures of different foods? Bananas? Raw carrots? Raisins? Tomato sauce? Make a pictorial chart showing the results.

Do all the children speak the same language? Do some of them know other languages? Make a block graph of the different languages spoken by the children in the class.

Book vocabulary

What you need
A good supply of books suitable for small children.

What to do
Teach the children the language of literacy as soon as you can. Of course many children learn it quite naturally at home, but for those who do not, the concepts of page, word, sentence, title and cover can be awe-inspiring. Every time you pick up a book to read a story or a poem, ask one of the children to turn the book the right way up, tell you what's on the 'cover', find the 'first page', help you with a 'sentence', look for a nice-to-say 'word'.

Allow the children to 'make friends' with books, with stories, with poems and with everything that is written. If you can teach them to love and welcome literature through your own enthusiasm, there will not be any need for them to be so afraid of words that they have to 'attack' them by artificial means!

Share the reading with them. Help them to anticipate and predict what might happen next; what the next word might be; how the story is going to end. Let them see themselves as 'real' readers. Read with them, not at them.

Can they show you:

- the first page of the book?
- the last page of the book?
- the top of the page?
- the bottom of the page?
- the front of the book?
- the back of the book?
- the beginning of the story?
- a word?
- a line?
- the words under the picture?
- the words over the picture?
- which word comes next?

Feelings and emotions

Chapter two

Encourage the children to talk about their feelings and emotions. How do you feel? What makes you feel good? What makes you feel bad? What makes you feel angry? What is it like when you feel angry? What makes you feel sad? What is it like when you feel sad? What makes you feel happy? What is it like when you feel happy? What does your face do when you're happy/sad/angry/upset/cross?

Exploring idioms

What you need
No special equipment.

What to do
Discuss with the children the different words and expressions for laughing and crying. How many words do the children know for laughing, such as: laugh, chuckle, giggle, laugh your head off, chuckle like a drain, die of laughter? Often they hear language around them that does not make any sense at all to their way of thinking.

Do they know the meaning of: weeping, sobbing, sniffling, wailing, blubbering, snivelling, floods of tears, burst into tears, crying one's eyes out?

Can they show you: a smile, a grimace, a frown, a scowl, a pout, a grin (like a Cheshire cat!), cheerfulness, sulkiness, grumpiness, moodiness, delight, joy, pleasure?

Masks

What you need
Paper plates, paint, brushes, paper, pen, string or wool, felt-tipped pens, cotton wool, fabric scraps, card, pipe-cleaners, ribbon.

What to do
Make paper-plate masks showing different moods. Ask the children to depict their own faces as happy, sad, angry, sulky etc.

Make small holes each side of the plate and thread through pieces of string, or wool, to tie the mask on to the child's head. Cut holes for eyes and paint 'mood' faces with felt-tipped pens or crayons. Stick on cotton wool, wool or bits of material for hair, make spectacles out of card or pipe-cleaners and add bits of ribbon or coloured paper to make bows and decorations.

Mount the masks on a wall and make a 'poem' out of them. For example:

- When Sarah has a birthday it makes her (put a happy face here).
- When Rashed has a tummy ache it makes him (put a grumpy face here).
- When Peter loses his sweets it makes him (put a sulky face here).
- When Sammy plays with her friends it makes her (put a cheerful face here).

Display as many masks as space will allow and then talk about the words that are missing. What are they? Point out to the children that there is not necessarily just one right answer. Cheerful can be swapped for happy, delighted and smiling; sulky can sometimes be exchanged for sad, unhappy, miserable and grumpy. Let the children decide. Aim to draw from them as many synonyms as possible. Help them to understand that one word might be as fitting as the others, that they can agree to differ and that they do not always have to choose the same word as everybody else.

Make masks of different characters, such as clowns, witches, pirates and animals, in fact any kind of identity you can think of which will aid role-play, imagination and language development.

All the time the children are making the masks they will be learning and practising new vocabulary. Give clear and precise instructions, one at a time. First, you must draw the face: what kind of face will it be? Where should the eyes be? The eyebrows? How shall we draw the nose? What about the mouth? Is it going to smile? Will it be open? Shall we stick on some teeth? How shall we do the hair? Should it be straight or curly? Shall we make a beard? A moustache? Shall we make a hat to stick on the head?

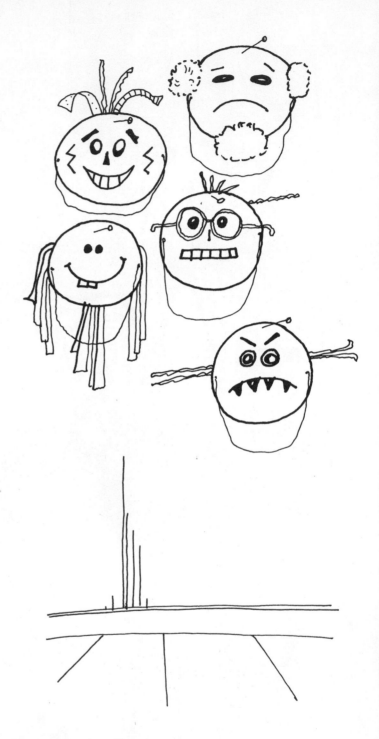

Paper bag puppets

Moods and emotions can be explored through puppets. They can be made very easily and offer enormous potential for language development. Small children have an almost magical affinity with them. With absolutely no inhibitions, children are able to make a mental leap straight out of their own lives into the life and being of the puppet and invent a vicarious existence that gives them undoubted satisfaction and an incredible facility for language development.

Puppet-making does not need to be complicated or arduous; children need only a symbol for their imagination to take flight!

What you need

Paper bags, scissors, cotton wool, card, feathers, adhesive, string, wool, scraps of fabric, paints or felt-tipped pens, elastic bands.

What to do

Stick cardboard ears on to the paper bags to make animals, or feathers to make birds. Bits of string or wool can be used for whiskers, chunks of cotton wool for noses and eyes, and bits of white card for teeth. A beak can be made by cutting out a triangle of card, folding it as in Figure 1 and sticking it on the bag.

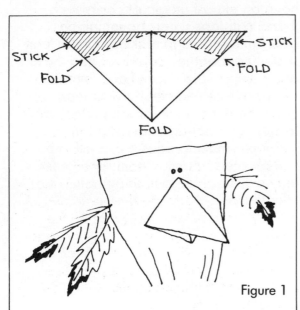

Figure 1

Make happy/sad faces by painting one side of the bag with a happy face and the other side with a sad face.

Begin by printing out the instructions for making the puppets on a large piece of card and read them out, instruction by instruction, with the children joining in. You can introduce lots of concepts by doing this: first, second, next etc. This will also familiarise the children with writing that is not from a story or a book. Point out that the instructions begin with a list of things that they need to have and use. Show them how the list works, that you read the instructions one at a time and that one instruction follows another.

Read through the whole set of instructions. Explain to the children that they should go back to the beginning of the list to check that they have all the items. Tell them that they do not have to remember everything at once but that they can accomplish one step before returning to the instructions to find out about the next.

By the time you have been through the instructions several times they will have 'learned' some of the words or phrases and should be able to pick them out easily.

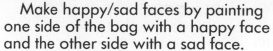

While the puppets are being made, encourage the children to make up their stories. What's your puppet's name? Is it a boy or a girl? Is it a child or an adult? Where has it come from? Where is it going? What is it going to wear? What has it got to do? Who are its friends? What games does it like to play? What does it eat? What stories does it know? What can it read? What will it say if I say hello to it?

Show the children how to put the paper bags over their wrists and how to secure them with elastic bands.

By the time the puppets are finished the children will have created whole stories for them. Ask them to work in pairs or small groups and explore the stories together. The value of this activity, of course, lies in the process of doing, talking and sharing, not in the creation of a beautifully-made model puppet.

Role-play

Chapter three

Lots of language can be developed from role-play, without a child even being aware of it. Set up different role-play situations through discussion. Allow the children to assume different roles and to dress up to enact those roles. Hats are particularly appropriate for role-play: once you put a postman's cap on everybody knows what you are! On the other hand, dressing-up clothes do not need to be elaborate — an old scarf or tea-towel tied round the head transforms a child into a pirate or a nurse. The clothing is merely a symbol that the child is no longer herself, thus inspiring her not to behave like herself or, even more to the point, not to talk in her usual way.

Let's celebrate

What you need
Dressing-up clothes, a doll, toy food.

What to do
Initiate the following discussions with the children.
● What shall we celebrate? Let's celebrate a new baby. The baby is coming home from hospital today. What shall we do to prepare for her? How shall we take care of her? What shall we go and buy for her? How will she be fed? How are we going to look after her? Who will do the jobs?
● What shall we celebrate? Let's celebrate a birthday. Today is somebody's birthday. What shall we do to mark the occasion? We can make birthday cards to send in the post. What do we need to make them? How shall we decorate them? How shall we get ready for the party? What shall we buy? What shall we make? Who shall we invite? What games shall we play?
● What shall we celebrate? Let's celebrate a wedding. Who is getting married? Who shall be the bride? Who shall be the bridegroom? Who shall be the bridesmaids and the pageboys? What do we need for dressing up? How shall we get ready for the wedding? What about the guests/presents/food for the party/clothes/invitations/make-up for the bride and bridesmaids? Who's going to make the cake?

Where shall we go?

What you need
Dressing-up clothes, blankets, bags, card, pencils.

What to do
Introduce the following role-play situations which explore activities unfamiliar to some children.

● Where shall we go? Let's go to the dentist. What's to be done? How do we look after our teeth? Who shall be the receptionist? The nurse? The dentist? What kind of things will they each need? Where shall we sit? What shall we do while we wait? What will happen when we get called in?

● Where shall we go? Let's go to the hospital. Who shall be the patients? The nurses and doctors? The visitors? What shall each person wear? What does each person need? What's wrong with the patients? How can we cheer them up? Talk about the daily routine in hospital, encourage the children to think about what happens before lunch, what happens after lunch, at what time the patients have tea, when it is time for them to go to sleep again.

● Where shall we go? Let's go on holiday. How shall we decide where to go? Who will come with us? Where shall we stay? How shall we travel? What shall we pack? What shall we do when we get there? Who shall we send postcards to? What shall we draw on the front? What shall we write on the back? How shall we post them? What will the people who receive them say? Who shall we buy presents for? What shall we buy?

Help the children to make books about the situations they have experienced.

A special day

What you need
A child who has been a bridesmaid or a pageboy at a wedding.

What to do
If one of the children has been a bridesmaid, help her to recount the experience to the rest of the class. Talk about the excitement she must have felt. Was she afraid of doing something wrong? Ask her to describe the wedding: who was getting married? Who else was at the wedding? What did they have to eat? What did they do at the reception? Did she see the presents?

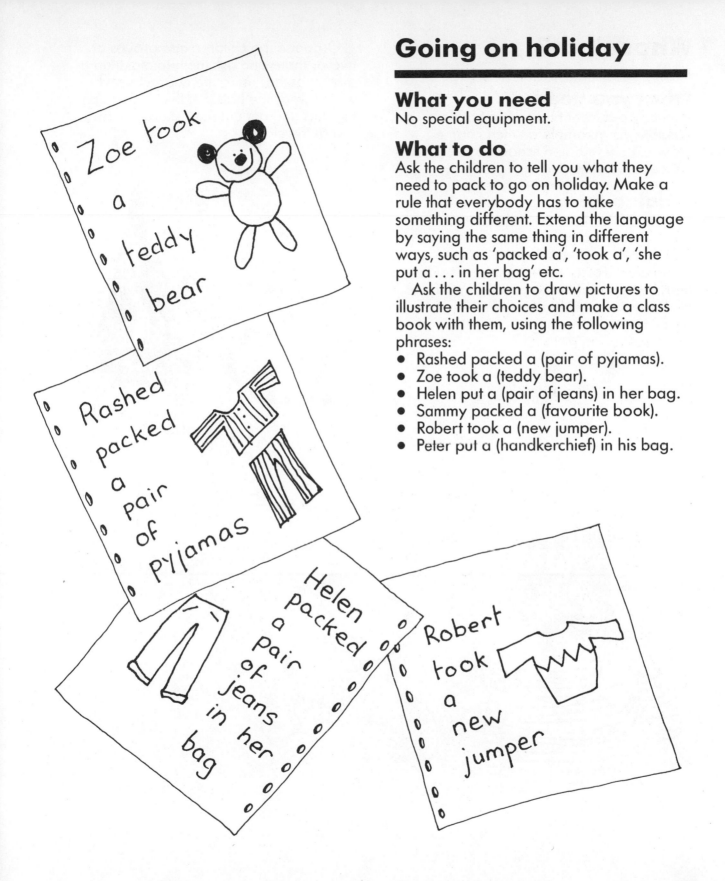

Going on holiday

What you need
No special equipment.

What to do
Ask the children to tell you what they need to pack to go on holiday. Make a rule that everybody has to take something different. Extend the language by saying the same thing in different ways, such as 'packed a', 'took a', 'she put a . . . in her bag' etc.

Ask the children to draw pictures to illustrate their choices and make a class book with them, using the following phrases:

- Rashed packed a (pair of pyjamas).
- Zoe took a (teddy bear).
- Helen put a (pair of jeans) in her bag.
- Sammy packed a (favourite book).
- Robert took a (new jumper).
- Peter put a (handkerchief) in his bag.

Zoe took a teddy bear

Rashed packed a pair of Pyjamas

Helen packed a pair of jeans in her bag

Robert took a new jumper

Whose hat?

What you need

As many different types of hat as possible, for example a witch's hat, a crown, a chef's hat, a schoolboy's cap, a policeman's helmet.

What to do

Let the children put on the different hats and ask them to act out the movements that the wearer would make. Introduce movement words; for example, a soldier marches and salutes, a policeman strides and directs the traffic, a chef stirs, whisks, beats and rolls.

Organise the children into groups of two or three and ask them to make up a story together using the characters who would wear the hats. Let them dress up in the hats and act out their stories to the rest of the class.

Books and pictures

Chapter four

The use of books and pictures can provide enormous scope for language development in the youngest children, from the moment they learn to recognise pictures of objects and articulate their names to when they first learn to recognise written words. Encourage the children to look at books and pictures and describe what they see and to make their own stories by drawing or cutting out pictures from magazines and writing their own captions for them.

This chapter contains activities which are all designed to help children turn what they see and experience into written and spoken words.

Looking at pictures

What you need
A selection of the children's own photographs.

What to do
Ask the children to bring in photographs of themselves in different situations, for example as babies, at their christening, at a party, being a bridesmaid etc. Encourage them to talk about what they were like in those situations and times. For example:
- When you were little you could not do the things that you can do now. What could you not do?
- What have you learned to do as you've grown?
- What do you think you might become good at as you get older?

Write your own books

What you need
Reading book, paper, felt-tipped pens.

What to do
Choose a strongly patterned book, for example *Brown Bear, Brown Bear, What Do You See?* by Bill Martin and Eric Carle (Picture Lions), and use it as a model for the class to make up its own story; for example:

'Purple pig, purple pig, what do you see?
I see a yellow goose looking at me.
Yellow goose, yellow goose, what do you see?
I see a striped sheep looking at me', etc.

Let the children decide together on the words. Print the words on large pages and let the children illustrate them. Then repeat the reading process as follows:

- Read the story to the group, pointing to each word.
- Get the children to chant the story with you.
- Let the children chant the story with minimal support.
- Let the children try to read the story themselves.
- Let the children read and share their own books in the leisure corner.

Pop-up books

What you need
Paper, pencil, felt-tipped pens, scissors, adhesive.

What to do
Fold a sheet of paper in half. Turn down a triangle from the folded edge and bend it backwards and forwards. Push the fold inwards.

Ask the children to draw a character from one of their own stories and colour it in. Cut out the picture then fold it down the centre with the coloured side outwards. Stick the picture on to the sheet of paper so that the fold is directly over the crease. When the page is folded and opened up again the figure will pop up.

Ask the children to make several pages in this way, then stick them together to form a story-book.

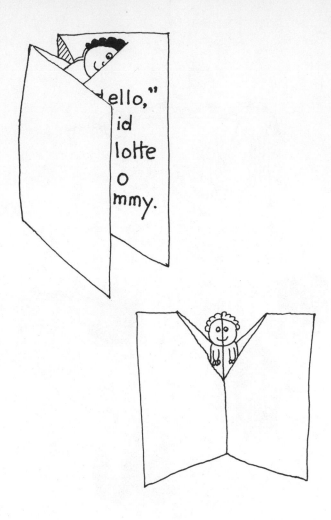

Making albums

What you need
Photographs, adhesive, sheets of A4 paper, pencils, felt-tipped pens, paints, paintbrushes.

What to do
Ask the children to draw, paint or crayon pictures of their photographs. Make 'albums' for each child, using A4 paper. Let the children express what is happening in the pictures. Let them scribble-write their own captions. Only decode if they really want you to.

The real language value is in the process of putting their thoughts and ideas into words, not in producing a beautiful piece of work (though that helps to motivate them, of course!).

Diary on the wall

What you need
Seven large sheets of paper, pen, stapler.

What to do
Keep a big weekly diary on the wall, using seven large sheets of paper. Ask the children if they can help you remember the names of the days of the week. Write one at the top of each sheet.

At the end of each day and every Monday morning have a discussion about the events of the day, or the weekend, and write or draw it up. Use the appropriate tenses of verbs, to help the children to acquire this crucial language skill.

Refer to the diary every day, introducing words such as 'yesterday', 'tomorrow', 'last week', 'next week' etc. At the end of each week, staple the pages together and display them in the leisure corner where the children can refer to them.

Mail-order catalogues

What you need
Mail-order catalogues, scissors, card, adhesive, various household objects and articles of clothing, paper, string, toy telephone.

What to do
Let the children look at a selection of mail-order catalogues. Talk to them about the pictures and encourage them to tell anecdotes about home that may be prompted by the pictures.

Let the children cut out a number of pictures that they particularly like. Discuss fully with each child the items depicted in the pictures. What are they? What colour are they? Who are they for? Who would like to buy them?

Make a card folder for each child with space for the picture and a piece of writing. Stick the pictures in place then ask the children to give you text to accompany the article. Let them suggest catalogue numbers and prices.

For each catalogue make an order form where the children can write their name, catalogue number and name of the article they want to order.

Extend this activity with role-play. Make parcels containing the kind of household objects, or articles of clothing, illustrated in the pictures. Get the children to 'order' the articles by 'post' or by 'telephone' and choose someone to act as the delivery person.

Personal books

What you need
Picture story books about going for a walk, card, adhesive tape, pencil, scissors, felt-tipped pens, ribbon, paper, hole punch.

What to do
Let the children share and discuss picture story books such as *Rosie's Walk* by Pat Hutchins (Bodley Head). Discuss walks that the children have to take, such as going to school or going to the shops. Encourage the use of phrases such as 'cross the road', 'over the bridge', 'under the underpass' or 'through the park'.

Let the children make their own books about going for a walk. Cut out two pieces of card for the front and back covers and let the children decorate them. Stick a smaller piece of card on to one of the covers to make a pocket.

Ask each child to make a drawing of himself on a piece of card, colour it and cut it out. Stick one end of a piece of ribbon on to the card figure and stick the other end on to the front cover, behind the pocket. Slip the figure into the pocket.

Give each child several sheets of paper slightly smaller than the card covers. Ask the children to draw a picture on each piece of paper showing a different stage of their walk. Write a short caption for each picture.

Put the books together by punching holes along the length of the paper and the card and secure by threading through a piece of ribbon.

When the books are finished, let the children retell their stories by walking the cardboard figure through the pages of their books.

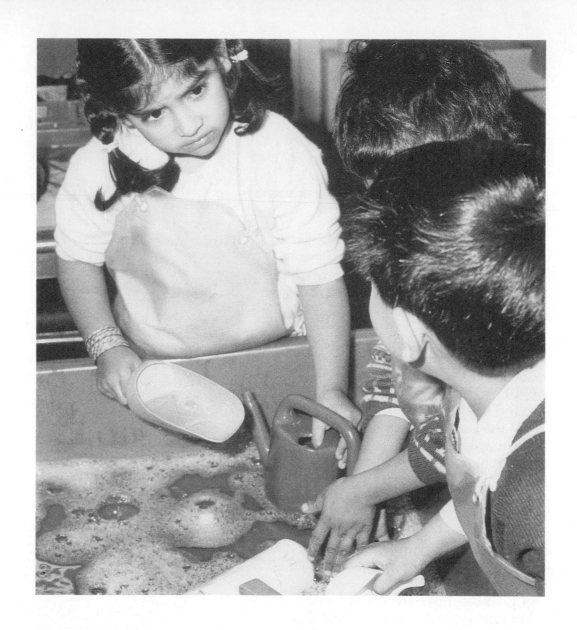

Sand and water

Chapter five

Playing with sand and water offers plenty of scope for the development of mathematical language, as well as introducing the concepts of volume, wet, dry, floating and sinking.

Sand play

What you need
Yoghurt and margarine pots, old dishes, spoons with holes in them, washing-up liquid bottles, containers, large boxes, labels, pens, sand, spoons, an assortment of small objects and toys.

What to do
Provide lots of containers, pourers, pots, dishes, spoons with holes in and yoghurt pots. Practically anything you can find around the home will be useful.

Let the storing of such material and equipment be a signpost to language development by having large boxes, carefully labelled, in a prominent place. Use the same phrases, so that when you have pointed the labels out to the children a few times they will be able to predict what they say. Stick on a picture of the item that goes in the box to cue them in to the word.

If possible, have two lots of sand available, one wet and one dry. Dry sand will behave in almost the same way as a liquid (apart from floating and sinking), but not in the same way as wet sand. Can the children make it drip? Trickle? Squirt? How does it act in your hands? Does it stay there, or does it run out through your fingers? Can it be squeezed, held, collected?

Use spoons to measure different quantities of sand. How many teaspoons of sand does it take to fill a yoghurt pot? How many tablespoons? If you fill one yoghurt pot with, for example, five teaspoons of sand and another one with

five tablespoons of sand, does one contain more than the other?

Make a set of balancing scales with margarine pots. Fill one side with sand. What happens to the other side? Put sand into the other side, watch for the pots to balance. What happens if you put in too much sand? What happens if you fill one side with sand and the other side with plastic cubes? How much sand would it take to balance a toy car?

Through this kind of play the children will practise maths language, including heavier than, lighter than, balancing, more than, less than and the same as.

Tables and lists

What you need
Yoghurt pot, sand, scales, objects for weighing, pen, paper.

What to do
Make tables and lists for the children to complete, as in Figure 1.

Completing the tables will of course need lots of help and guidance. Have the children read the instructions with you several times. Give them plenty of picture cues and oral assistance and ask them to 'read' the words to you as often as possible. Keep their writing task to a minimum; they need only tick or illustrate the answer they think appropriate. This activity will help to familiarise them with the written symbols for particular words and with the idea of lists and tables. Also, keeping a record will give their findings importance.

These things weigh the same as one yoghurt pot full of sand.

	Yes	No
Two crayons	✓	
Four cubes	✓	
A piece of sponge	✓	
An apple	✓	

These things weigh less than a yoghurt pot full of sand.

	Yes	No
A pencil	✓	
A glove	✓	
A peg	✓	
An orange	✓	

Figure 1

Water play

What you need
A variety of containers and utensils, toys that float, water, pen, paper.

What to do
Collect together objects for the water corner which will provide a variety of experiences. Include containers that hold water; that squirt and pour; sieves and colanders; materials that can be squeezed; that will float; that will sink; objects used for stirring and for whisking.

Again, make storage of the materials part of the language development programme.

Aim to give the children the kind of experiences that will lead to words like: trickle, stream, pour, splash, splatter, plop, soak, wring, squeeze, float, sink, still, waves, smooth, slippery, warm and cold.

Complete a list

What you need

A variety of objects that float, sink, hold water, let it through, squirt and pour; pen, paper.

What to do

Allow the children to experiment with floating objects in water. Include items such as a wooden boat, a cork, a pebble, a shell, a sponge and a rubber ball.

Provide pictures of all these objects and ask the children to compile pictorial

These things float

These things sink

lists under the headings 'These things float' and 'These things sink'.

Repeat the experiment with objects that hold water and those that let it through. Include objects such as a spoon, a spatula, a colander, a sponge, a glove and a shell.

Repeat the experiment a third time, using objects that squirt and pour water. Include items such as a washing-up liquid container, a watering can and a jug.

Encourage the children to find out what are the objects from which you can wring out the water. For example, use a flannel, a piece of wood, a sponge, a piece of modelling clay and a glove.

Make a water book

What you need
Paper, felt-tipped pens.

What to do
Compile a 'water book' for the children with an illustrated page for each discovery; for example, water is wet; sometimes water is cold; sometimes water is warm.

For each page the children need to have lots of experience of water play, followed by discussion. How do you know water is wet? What does wet feel like? What else is wet? When is water cold? What about the rain? What does rain feel like on your hands? When is water warm? When is water hot? What do we use hot water for? What happens if we colour the water with food colouring? Does it behave in the same way as ordinary water? Go through all the experiments together in small groups and find out if the sinking, floating, pouring and containing results are the same for each group.

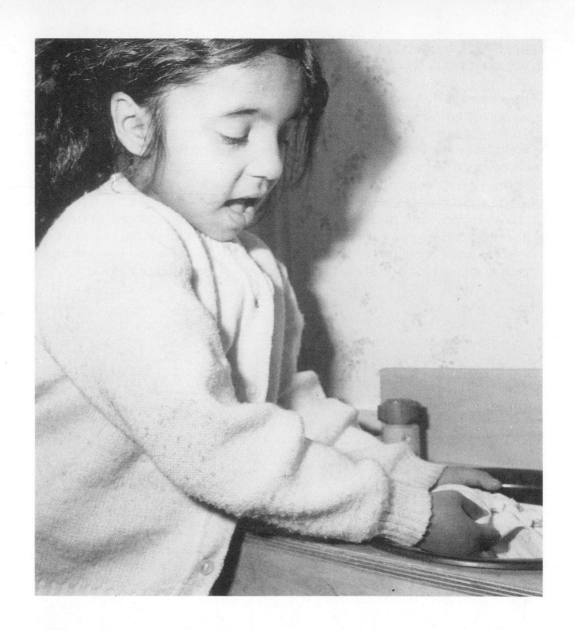

The home corner

Chapter six

Even if you do not have a home corner in the classroom, it is very easy to set one up. All you need are two or three chairs with a blanket thrown over them to make a sofa, a little table, something on the floor for a carpet, various toys such as an ironing board, a cupboard, a telephone, a set of keys. Make a sink out of a cardboard box with cut-out card taps; use upturned boxes for furniture; make an oven by painting rings on one end of a box and cutting a door that opens into one side; paint a picture of a window, attach curtains to it and stick it to the wall so that it becomes the 'wall' of the house. The one thing that small children have in abundance is imagination!

Make sure the house has reading and writing materials in it. Include books, comics, magazines, catalogues, letters, birthday cards, shopping lists and telephone messages. In order to have the children behaving like real readers and writers give them the opportunity to imitate grown-up behaviour.

Play in the house or home corner can be directed towards number and vocabulary tasks.

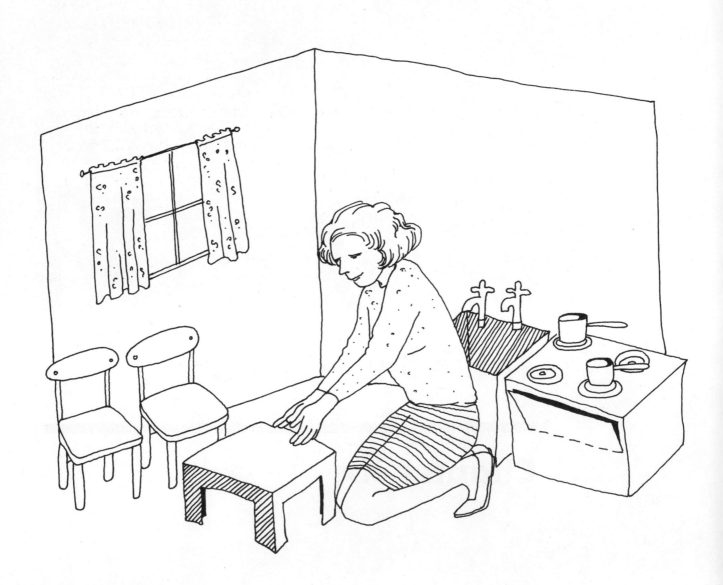

Be a family

What you need

Table, chairs, toy tea-set, scissors, card, felt-tipped pens.

What to do

Ask the children to imagine that they are a family at home. How many people live in the house? Who are they? Who is the oldest? Who is the youngest? What jobs have to be done in the house? Who does them? Who is coming to visit? How will you welcome them? Lay the table for tea. How many people will there be? How many cups? How many saucers? How many spoons?

Make some cakes for the visitors. What kind of cakes will you make? What will you need to make them? How will you measure the ingredients? What will you mix them with? How will you decorate them? Draw the cakes on card and cut them out. Lay the table with two cakes for each person. How many cakes will you need altogether?

Do the shopping

What you need
Paper, pencils.

What to do
Another game for the 'family' to play is shopping. Choose a different child to do the shopping for each day of the week. Repeat the days of the week several times. Have the children decide what to buy for each day. Encourage them to write a shopping list:

Monday   Fish and chips
Tuesday   Sugar and potatoes
Wednesday   Bananas and ice-cream

   Is the shopping going to be heavy or light to carry? Will you need a shopping bag or can you manage with your hands? How much money will you need? Will you have any change left over?

   Make up a song for everyone to sing at the end of the game. For example:
'On Monday I went shopping and I bought some fish, bought some fish, bought some fish;
On Monday I went shopping and I bought some fish, then I ate it all up for my tea.'

   Repeat the song with the items listed for each day of the week.

Tidying up

What you need
Miscellaneous objects from the home corner, teddy bears, paint, paper.

What to do
Find lots of different ways to tidy up. Ask the children to put something underneath something; something on top of something; something in front of something; something behind something; something opposite something; something over something; something at the side of something.

Extend the use of this vocabulary by tidying up the classroom in the same way. Place teddy bears in different areas and ask the children where they are, encouraging them to use the place words they have learned.

Paint pictures of the teddies in different positions: on top of the cupboard, behind the clock, at the side of the blocks, inside a box, in front of the door. When the pictures are finished, display them on the wall, with the words clearly written: 'Can you see Teddy (behind the clock)?'. Read the sentences several times over with the children until they can join in.

Telephone calls

What you need
A toy telephone, pencil, note pad.

What to do
Ask the children to make 'telephone calls' to the doctor, the dentist, the flower shop, granny etc. Can you make an emergency telephone call? Can you give your name and address clearly? Can you make an appointment on the telephone to see the doctor? Can you take a message for someone else in the house? Write down the appointments and messages on the telephone pad.

Sewing

What you need
Card, pen, hole punch, large needle, coloured wool.

What to do
Draw simple shapes on card and punch holes around the edges. Use large, thick needles and brightly coloured wool. Show the children how to take the thread through and up and down and in the front, as well as over the back of the card.

Baby-sitting

What you need
Dolls, teddy bears, dolls' clothes.

What to do
Let the dolls and teddies be part of the family, needing to be talked to, dressed, fed and put to bed. Let the children find clothes that are too big, too small and just the right size. Ask them for clothes that have zips, buttons, press-studs and toggles.

Use sorting and matching activities: have the children find all the items that are for dressing; for putting on the beds and cots; for doing jobs around the house. Let them find all the things in the house that are red, blue etc.

Organising a party

What you need

Paper, felt-tipped pens, scissors, card.

What to do

Decide whose birthday it is going to be and discuss the party arrangements. Who shall be invited?

Ask the children to design some special birthday-party invitation cards, write them and post them in the classroom post-box. Choose someone to be the postman to deliver the cards to the children.

Make some paper or card jam tarts and a birthday cake, lay out the table and find something to wrap up for a present. What games will you play at the birthday party?

Weather

Chapter seven

The themes of weather and the seasons offer numerous opportunities for language development and can incorporate work on trees, plants, birds and seasonal games and activities. Take the children for walks outside or organise outside play sessions to experience as many different weather conditions as possible.

There are all kinds of weather activities you can do, both inside the classroom and out of doors.

Out of doors

What you need
No special equipment.

What to do
Talk about the seasons. Most of the children will have started school in the autumn but may not yet be aware of the changing patterns of the seasons.

They will remember the sunny days of summer, going on holiday, having time to play and older children not being at school. Can you remember what the grass was like, how the flowers bloomed, how much gardening there was to do? Do you remember if the sky was blue or very cloudy? Did it rain very much? Was it warm or cold? What kind of clothes did you wear? What did you wear on your feet?

What is different now? What does the grass look like? What about the trees? The sky? Is the weather any different? What do we need to wear outdoors? Why do we wear different clothes in autumn? Where are all the flowers? Are there any fruits on the trees and bushes?

Seasonal collections

What you need
Display materials, pencils, paper, books, blotting paper, clear self-adhesive plastic film.

What to do
Collect and display various seasonal objects. For example, in autumn collect conkers, acorns, sprigs of blackberry, different leaves and seeds. In the summer collect and press common wildflowers such as dandelions and daisies. Explain to the children why they should not pick the less common plants.

Allow the children to draw what they saw and collected. With the children, write some words to describe the display. Discuss the words and write them out for the children. Ask the children questions. What shall we write? Did anything happen on our trip that we would like to tell everyone about? Shall we describe the weather or what the trees and leaves looked like? By involving the children in the message-making, letting them all have some ownership of it, you allow them to absorb an awareness of written language as communication, as important and meaningful.

Make up a poem or a story to go with your display. It does not have to be long or complicated, in fact the simpler the better. Give it a word or rhythm pattern so that the children can learn it easily. If they can do actions to it, so much the better. Children love funny rhymes that have something about themselves in them.

If you do these kinds of activity at the beginning of every season you will help the children to assimilate the idea of change.

What's the weather like?

What you need
Pen, paper, felt-tipped pens.

What to do
Keep a weather chart or diary in the classroom, including the children's own painting, drawing, colouring etc. Reinforce the pattern of the days of the week by daily changing the display.

When it is raining, discuss the weather with the children. Is it drizzling? Spotting? Pouring down? Lashing the windows? Bouncing off the playground? When is rain just a passing shower? When is it a downpour?

What does the sky look like? What shape are the clouds? Are they soft and fluffy? White? Smooth and grey? Black and heavy?

Is there a rainbow? What can the children tell you about a rainbow? How many colours make up a rainbow? Which colour is on the outside? Which colour is on the inside? What shape is the rainbow? Where do you think it ends? What do you think it is made of? Together, make up a story or a poem about rainbows. Make a class book about rain.

It's snowing!

What you need
Paper, paints, brushes, pencils.

What to do
Snow, of course, is the magic weather condition! If possible, go outside while it is falling and let the children try to catch it in their hands, on their fingers, on their tongues. What does it feel like on your hands? On your face? On your tongue? Can you catch it? Can you hold it? What happens when it touches your warm skin? What makes it melt? How does it fall? Does it pour? Does it shower? Does it drift? Float? Dance in the air? What does a snowflake look like? Is it dull? Is it shiny? Does it sparkle? Can you paint one?

Talk about what the children can do when the snow has settled, such as building snowmen, making giant

snowballs and snow castles. These are all activities designed for doing first and then talking, writing and painting about.

Make up your own snow rhymes with the children. Choose a rhyme they know well with a strong rhythm or word pattern. Put new words to the pattern after the 'snow' experience. Write the poem up and display it on the wall, where they can all 'read' it to you, to each other, to visitors and to themselves.

For example, with lots of enthusiasm and encouragement the children can easily change 'Twinkle, twinkle, little star' into:
'Sparkle, sparkle, flake of snow
How I wonder where you go —
You dance and drift and when you land
You disappear upon my hand.'

The whole point is to keep the vocabulary simple. Guide the children with an easy but effective idea (in this case snow melting) and they will be so taken with having written their own poem that they will learn to recite and read it with hardly any help from you! Self-motivated practice is what makes successful readers!

Sparkle, sparkle, flake of snow,

How I wonder where you go.

You dance and drift and when
you land

You disappear upon my hand.

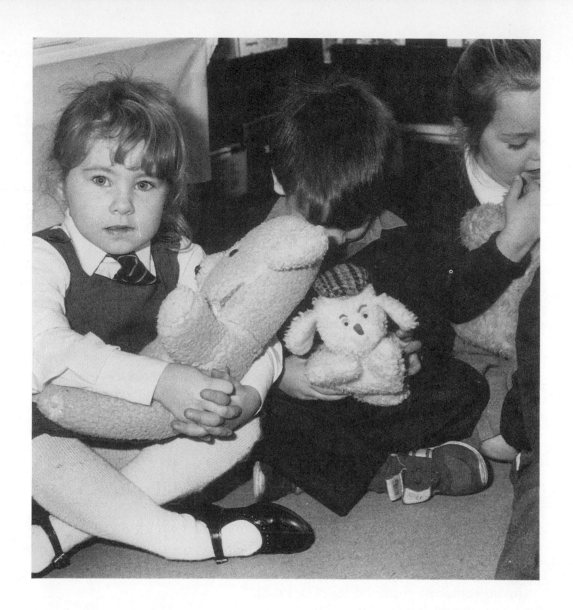

Animals

Chapter eight

Young children have a natural affection for and curiosity about animals. Looking after animals in the classroom teaches them a lot about growth, caring and responsibility. It is possible to get an enormous amount of language development out of keeping a classroom pet. A project about zoo animals can be used to introduce more imaginative language.

Classroom pets

What you need
Classroom pet, animal pictures and poems, a visitor from a pet shop or animal charity.

What to do
The children will enjoy the challenge of naming their classroom pet. They will also have to feed it, keep it clean and make sure it has suitable exercise. Plan a proper rota so that everyone has a 'turn' in looking after it. This kind of activity leads easily into work on the children's own pets and stimulates a lot of interest. Look out for pictures and poems which the children can share and enjoy together.

Invite someone from the local pet shop or from one of the animal caring organisations to talk to the children. Often they will bring with them some animals to show the children.

Create a zoo

What you need
Soft toys, copies of photocopiable pages 94 and 95, paper, scissors, felt-tipped pens, card, cardboard box, clear acetate film, silver foil, rod, thread, books about animals.

What to do
Ask the children to bring in all the soft toys and other toy animals that they can. Be prepared for a deluge!

Make paper snakes by cutting spirals out of paper and colouring them in (Figure 1). Use photocopiable page 94 as a template. String them across the

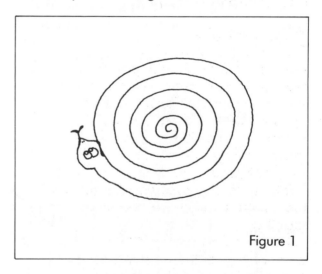

Figure 1

room to make a Snake House for your zoo. Make paper monkeys using photocopiable page 95, and suspend them from the ceiling.

Ask the children to sort the toys into sets, such as elephants, big cats, bears, monkeys, seals and dolphins etc. If you do not have some species, make them out of card and paint them.

Talk about how the animals will be kept in your zoo. Organise different habitats and cages for different kinds of animal. Arrange the classroom so that there is plenty of room for a day or two and let your zoo take over. Make labels for the different areas such as Giraffe Enclosure, Monkey House, Reptile House etc.

Build cages and dens out of card. Make an aquarium out of a cardboard box, cut out the sides and cover them with transparent paper. Make beautifully coloured paper fish with silvery scales and hang them from a rod across the top of the aquarium.

Make labels and notices for the zoo. 'Please do not feed the monkeys.' 'Danger! This lion is fierce. Don't poke your fingers in the cage!' 'Warning! This hippo is always hungry!' Get the children to talk about the notices and write them out together.

Arrange the animals in their respective habitats, making sure that they have the right kind of environment (made out of paper or card). The children can find out what they need to make by researching in books.

Beware of the lion.

Do not feed the animals

Zoo day

What you need
Paper, pencils, felt-tipped pens, paints, paintbrushes.

What to do
Transform the classroom door into the zoo entrance and put up a notice stating how much it costs to come in. Make entrance tickets showing the price. Choose a zoo-keeper, or two (and change them often so that everyone gets a turn!).

Invite people to visit your zoo. Have two children selling tickets so that one is collecting the money and adding it up (any real money can go to an animal charity or to buy some animal books for the book corner!). The children can show the visitors round, pointing out the various species and imparting their knowledge about feeding and caring.

When the zoo closes

What you need
Paint, paintbrushes, paper, tape recorder, camera.

What to do
Wind up the whole exercise with discussion sessions. The children will have enjoyed the experience enormously and can record their enjoyment in various ways. Some may want to paint pictures of what they liked best, some may want to make a zoo book with your help, others may like to tape-record their own stories of the zoo.

Take lots of photographs and make a large book to help them assimilate everything that happened.

Listening

Chapter nine

All the activities in this chapter involve sounds, either verbal or musical, and encourage children to listen carefully to what they hear. Children love to make music, and it is a good way of getting them to develop their concentration and listening skills.

kind of sound does the instrument make? Can you make loud sounds and quiet sounds? Can you make heavy sounds and light sounds? Which instrument would you use to make an elephant's music? A teddy bear's music? A squeaky little gerbil's music?

Making music

What you need
A variety of junk materials and craft materials for making percussion instruments.

What to do
You do not need to have lots of musical instruments; you can make your own quite easily.

Use a combination of the following ideas to make different sounds:
● Clap two yoghurt pots together, or tap sticks together;
● Put some seeds or pebbles into a yoghurt pot. Stick another pot firmly on the top with adhesive tape and use as a shaker;
● Fill bottles and jars with different levels of water and hit them with pencils or bits of dowelling;
● String milk-bottle tops together, tie them to a stick and use them as a shaker;
● Fix string or elastic bands tautly to sticks or blocks of wood and pluck them;
● Find different-sized closed containers and bang them with drumsticks;
● Scratch your fingers on a tin tray;
● Stick sandpaper to blocks and rub them together;
● Using string, hang eight wooden strips of different lengths from a stick and pull a dowel across them;
● Tap different pieces of wood together.

Ask the children to demonstrate the sounds and then to describe them. What do you have to do to make them? What

Build a sound story

What you need
Musical instruments, pen, paper.

What to do
Let the children help you make up a story with lots of sound effects in it, such as weather or animal noises, and set up an 'orchestra' to provide them. The children will have to choose which sounds go with each bit of the story, and whoever's turn it is will have to listen very carefully for her cue to come in.

When you have been over the story several times, letting each child have a go, write it out in bold letters with illustrations. Let the children read it out loud with you, making the sound effects where necessary.

Singing games

What you need
No special equipment.

What to do
Introduce singing games where the children carry out actions, for example:
'I'm a little teapot, short and stout,
Here's my handle, here's my spout,
When the water's ready, hear me shout
"Tip me up and pour me out".'

Play games where the children repeat the words after you, for example:
'One, two, three, four, five – once I caught a fish alive.
Six, seven, eight, nine, ten – then I threw him back again.'

Repeating games

What you need
No special equipment.

What to do
Hold up a finger and say, 'Here is one little finger and it goes tap.' Ask the children to repeat the phrase. Continue by saying 'Here are two little fingers and they go tap, tap.' Ask the children to repeat, and so on.

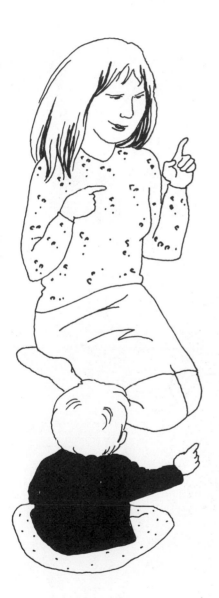

Going on a journey

What you need
No special equipment.

What to do
Tell the children that they are going on a trip and have to take a suitcase. You will take some of them with you, but only if they pack the right things. The children who can go on the trip are those who are able to name objects that begin with the initial sound of their name.

Tell the children to listen carefully. Say, 'My name is Mrs Jones (or whatever). I'm going on a trip and into my suitcase I'm packing a jacket.'

Ask each player what he will take along. For example, Samantha might say, 'My name is Samantha. I'm going on a trip and into my suitcase I'll pack some socks.'

You will reply, 'You may come.'

Rakesh might say, 'My name is Rakesh, I'm going on a trip and into my suitcase I'll pack a shirt.'

'I'm sorry,' you will reply, 'You must stay home during this trip.'

Make sure you play again so that the children who were not successful the first time have a second chance at the journey!

Listening game

What you need
Percussion instruments.

What to do
Collect or make simple percussion instruments. Give each child an instrument. Ask one child to beat out a rhythm then point to someone else to copy it on her instrument. If she gets the rhythm right, let her make up a rhythm and continue the game.

Simon says

What you need
No special equipment, percussion instruments for variation.

What to do
Stand in front of the group with the children facing you and as far apart from each other as space permits.

Tell the children that you are going to give them a number of commands which they must only obey when you precede them with, 'Simon says'. For example, when you say 'Simon says, wiggle your fingers' the children must copy. If you give an instruction without saying 'Simon says . . .', anybody who obeys is 'out'.

Introduce lots of new vocabulary with this game, such as body parts or action words (eg leap, squat, grin). When you use a new word match your command with an action. Don't try to 'fool' the children until the new word is established.

Variation
Give everyone a percussion instrument, and keep two for yourself, one of which is 'Simon'. When you play a rhythm on 'Simon' everyone must copy it, but if you play on the other instrument anyone who copies it is 'out'!

And then . . .

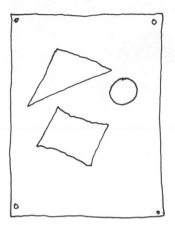

What you need
No special equipment.

What to do
Sit the children in a circle. Start telling a simple story, for example, 'One sunny day Jaswinder went shopping for her Mum. She put on her coat and then . . .'. Choose a child to compose and narrate the next bit of the story. When that child gets to 'and then', move on to another child, until the story is completed and all the children have had a turn.

Coffeepot

What you need
No special equipment.

What to do
Ask one child to stand apart from the class while the rest of the group decides on an action word (verb), for instance 'run'. Ask the first child to ask questions to try to find out what the verb is, using the word 'coffeepot' in its place.

'Can I coffeepot?' 'Yes.'

'Do I coffeepot at school?' 'Sometimes.'

'Does everybody coffeepot?' 'Sometimes.'

Of course, at this stage of development the children will enjoy making wild guesses but this all adds to the fun (and the vocabulary!).

Coffeepot-ly!

What you need
No special equipment.

What to do
Divide the class into two teams. The game requires one team to guess 'how' an action is being performed.

Let one team select an adverb, for example 'quietly'. The children in the other team ask the first team to perform tasks in the manner of the adverb such as walk like it, talk like it, until they guess the right word. Once the adverb has been guessed, let the teams swap over.

Next word

What you need
No special equipment.

What to do
Divide the children into teams. Begin to read a story aloud, pausing every so often in the middle or towards the end of a sentence to ask each team in turn, 'Next word?'. Give points for acceptable answers. The team with the most points at the end of the story wins.

Numbers

What you need
No special equipment.

What to do
Ask the children to stand up around the room. When you call out 'Mix into twos', let them form pairs. Anyone who does not have a partner must drop out.

Then call out, 'Mix into threes' and let the children scurry round to make sets of three. Again, anyone left over is out.

Continue calling out as far as the children have got with recognising numbers.

The game stops when there are too many children 'out' to count.

Words and pictures

Chapter ten

Visual stimulation plays an important part in a child's language development. All the activities in this chapter involve language work using visual images, either through pictures, observation or description.

What's in the bag?

What you need
A bag, several small objects.

What to do
Show the children five or six small objects and allow them to handle them. Put the objects in a bag so that the children cannot see them. Place your hand in the bag, take hold of one of the objects and describe what you are holding. Ask the children to work out what the object is. The child who guesses correctly then has a turn at describing an object, and so on.

I'm thinking of a colour

What you need
No special equipment.

What to do
Let one child select an object and whisper to you what it is. The child then says to the class, 'I'm thinking of something in this room and it is red.' The other children have to identify the object by asking questions, but the answer can only be yes or no. Encourage them not just to guess 'Is it the door?', but to ask more open-ended questions such as 'Is it something to wear?' or 'Is it on the floor?'.

Picture partners

What you need
Card, scissors, felt-tipped pens.

What to do
Make cards, each with a picture showing an item that forms a set, for example, a shopping bag, a shop and a purse; a cup, a saucer and a teaspoon; a dog, a dog's lead, and a bone.

Make sure that there are three items for every 'set'. Deal the cards at random to the children. Make a rule that the children can only talk to one child at a time and that they must not tell another person what somebody else's picture is, then ask them to sort themselves out into sets.

Acting nursery rhymes

What you need
No special equipment.

What to do
Divide the class into small groups and help each group to choose a nursery rhyme. Ask the children in each group to act out the rhyme using only mime and dialogue, not the actual words of the rhyme.

Work out actions to go with favourite nursery rhymes. Encourage the children to listen closely to the words of the rhyme and perform the actions at the right time. Discuss what the rhymes are saying and allow the children to make suggestions for movements.

For example, with 'Little Miss Muffet', get the children to make scooping movements to begin with, so that they are eating in time to the rhythm of the rhyme. Ask them to curl up small to be the spider lying in wait and then uncurl slowly, stretch out and scurry away on hands and feet.

For 'Twinkle, twinkle, little star' get the children to start from a curled position and make sharp jerky movements with their hands as they unfold and stretch themselves into star shapes. Organise them into a pattern of stars, some moving and some still, then work out a sequence to fit the rhyme.

For 'Hey diddle diddle' ask the children to make cat shapes — curling and stretching — leaping movements and laughing gestures, and finally forming pairs and dancing, holding hands as the dish and the spoon.

Jigsaw pictures

What you need
Old magazines and catalogues, scissors, card, adhesive.

What to do
Cut out and mount on to card big coloured pictures from magazines, catalogues etc. Cut them into four or five irregular pieces and ask the children to put them together to make a picture. When the picture is whole again ask them to describe what it is about.

Uncover a story

What you need
A poster or picture, pieces of paper, Blu-tak.

What to do
While the children are out of the room, put a picture up on the wall and cover it with pieces of paper.

Ask the children to sit on the floor near the picture. Take the pieces of paper off the picture one at a time and ask the children to predict what the picture will be.

Mixed up

What you need
No special equipment.

What to do
Divide the children into two teams. Ask one team to leave the room once they have had a very good look round it.

Tell the second team that it is the 'Mixer-upper' group and ask it to mix up as many things as possible, such as swapping one shoe, exchanging jumpers, moving places, turning things upside down etc. Let the first team come back in and ask it to look round and describe all the changes.

Smile, please!

What you need
Camera, film, card, materials for display, pen.

What to do
When the children are involved in a group activity, take photographs recording their progress. For example, if you go on a class outing, take pictures of the children getting ready, leaving the building, on the coach, arriving at their destination, having their lunch etc.

Back in the classroom, display the photographs out of sequence where all the children can see them. Encourage lots of talk about their shared activities. Ask the children to arrange the pictures in the sequence that tells the story of their outing.

Mount the photographs on sheets of card and ask the class to help you make up a caption for each one.

Show and tell

What you need
No special equipment.

What to do
Ask one child to bring an object from home which he can show and describe to the rest of the class. Group the children around him on the floor and let him choose his own words to describe the object. Only prompt him if he asks you for help.

Encourage good listening and attention skills among the other children, and at the end of the session choose someone else to be speaker for the next day.

After several sessions the children will be able to run 'show and tell' without any help from you.

Create a zoo, see page 69

Book list

Ten, Nine, Eight Molly Bang (Julia MacRae/Puffin)
Jack and the Robbers Val Biro (Oxford University Press)
The Story of the Dancing Frog Quentin Blake (Picture Lions)
Moo, Baa, La, La, La Sandra Boynton (*Boynton Board Books*, Methuen)
The Snowman Board Books Raymond Briggs (Hamish Hamilton)
A Walk in the Park Anthony Browne (Hamish Hamilton/Macmillan)
The Julian Stories Ann Cameron (Gollancz/Fontana Lions)
Dear Zoo Rod Campbell (Blackie/Puffin)
The Bad-Tempered Ladybird Eric Carle (Hamish Hamilton/Puffin)
Hairy Maclary Scattercat; Hairy Maclary's Bone Lynley Dodd (Spindlewood/Puffin)
The Patchwork Quilt Valerie Flournoy (Bodley Head/Puffin)
What Happens Next? Bill Gillham (Methuen)
Arthur Amanda Graham (Puffin)
It's Your Turn, Roger! Susanna Gretz (Bodley Head/Picture Lions)
The *Spot* series, Eric Hill (Heinemann/ Puffin)
When we went to the park Shirley Hughes (Walker)
Rosie's Walk; The Very Worst Monster; Don't Forget the Bacon; Titch Pat Hutchins (Bodley Head/Puffin)
Brown Bear, Brown Bear, What Do You See? Bill Martin and Eric Carle (Picture Lions)
This Little Puffin edited by Elizabeth Matterson (Puffin)
Reading Jan Ormerod (Walker)
Where the Wild Things Are Maurice Sendak (Bodley Head/Puffin)
Whose Footprints? Masayuki Yabuuchi (Bodley Head)

Books for teachers

What Did I Write? Marie Clay (Heinemann)
What's Whole in Whole Language? Ken Goodman (Scholastic)
The Craft of Children's Writing Judith Newman (Scholastic)
Read With Me Liz Waterland (Thimble Press)
A very useful guide to the best new children's books is *Signal*, which is available from the Thimble Press, Lockwood, Station Road, South Woodchester, Stroud, Glos. GL5 5QE.